Above: In the hopeful days, the line-up of rolling stock at Strabane in September 1964, with the two locos behind on the left. This is now the site of the Tinnies in 2018. Photo by the late Alan Tee.

Below: Stranorlar Station in 1971, now disappeared. This was demolished only a year or so later losing one of the most characterful buildings of CDR railway heritage. Photo by Neil Tee.

Above: Railcar 16 in the old railway yard at Stranorlar in 1971, see page 98 for pictures eight years earlier. Invisible behind the Railcar 16 tractor unit is the articulated trailer of Railcar 15 which was attached to it. This passenger carrying part of Railcar 15 still survives at Donegal Town but Railcar 16's tractor unit has disappeared as have all the yard buildings at Stranorlar. Note the single-deck bus in CDR colours. Photo by Neil Tee.
Below: The attractive station at Raphoe that was demolished for no apparent reason, despite attempts to save it, in the early 2000s. Photo by Neil Tee.

Michael Bunch's
Donegal
Railway
Diary
Part Two 1956-2018

Photographs (except where noted)
and original diary material
by Michael Bunch
Editing, captions and additions
by Neil Tee.

ISBN 978-1-874518-07-5

Above: A rare composite view of Victoria Road Station in Derry taken some time in the late 1960s showing the sloping covered ramp leading down from the booking hall to the platforms. The last CDR train to here was on 30th June 1955 but the station was resurrected a few years later. There was some activity from late 1974 by Donegal rolling stock and railcars over about 100 yards of track before these were shipped to Shane's Castle under the auspices of Lord O'Neill. It was when his operations ceased at Shane's Castle that items were brought back to the then new Foyle Valley Railway Museum built on the opposite side of the Foyle from here - see inside front cover. This was itself once the setting for the GNR broad gauge until its own closure in 1965. We have done our best to edit the pictures so that they blend together properly. Editing by Tony Maguire.

Below: A guide to the extent of the County Donegal Railway in 1927 when it was still at its peak which will help give context to the pictures in this part of Michael Bunch's Diary. A larger version of this map appears on the inside rear cover of Part 1. The map was kindly lent by Mr John Langford.

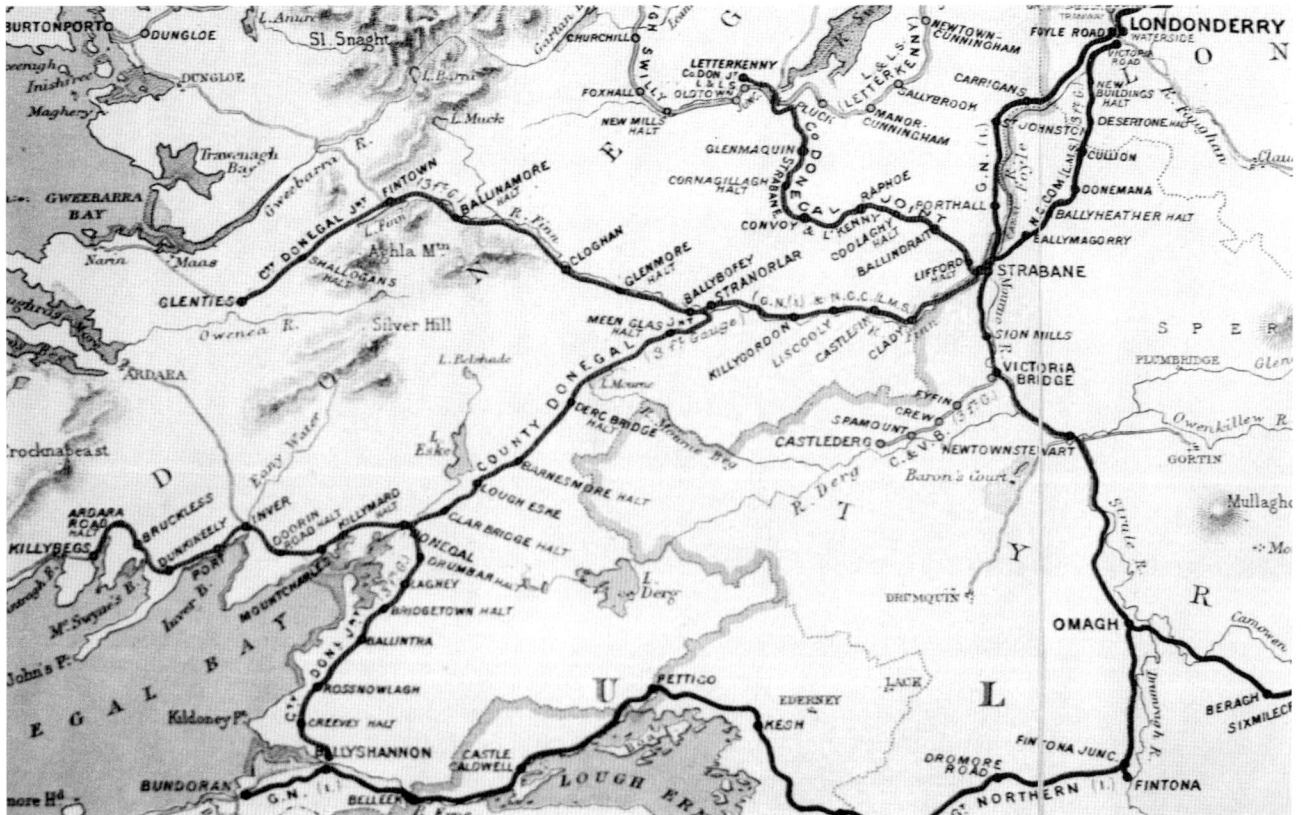

CONTENTS
(Relevant dates in left column)

Photographs in each section were taken on the date for that section
All photographs taken by Michael Bunch except where noted

Above: A view of the North West of Ireland's revived County Donegal operation in the late 1970s at Victoria Road Station in Derry. Railcar 12 is on the left and gave rides over the track which led via the point to two sidings. Red Van 19 stands off the track to the right. See page 110 onwards for a review of the various attempts to revive the County Donegal Railway. Photo by George Haire.

Preface

Michael Bunch, now in his mid eighties, and Neil Tee, aged 70, have co-operated together to create two books of comprehensively captioned photographs of the County Donegal Railway alongside Michael's own diary notes made at the same time the photographs were taken. Michael served five years in the UK Royal Air Force in the 1950s the last two being in Derry where he was able to exercise his life-long interest in railways by taking pictures of the Great Northern Railway (GNR) line and in particular the County Donegal Railway.

Michael also took pictures of these railways on all his subsequent visits to Derry and the sum total of these has provided the material for the books, the first, Michael Bunch's Donegal Railway Diary Part One 1954-55, and now this follow up, Part Two 1956-2008 with the remaining photos. While individual examples of Michael's photos had been published before, they had never been published as a collection in date order with Michael's diary text and detailed researched captions by Neil Tee, who has been associated with the preservation of both memories and artefacts of the line for over 25 years.

In Part Two the pictures cover the period from the County Donegal Railway (CDR) line being fully active to its demise and closure. The photos incorporate some unique last scenes of loco Erne in steam on the lifting train in 1960. We have included some associated pictures taken by Michael's long term acquaintance David Hyson and a few colour shots of the demise of the line taken by Neil Tee.

There are also some photos kindly contributed by George Haire from his archives. A native of Strabane, George has for many years studied and lectured on the history of the CDR. George and Neil have worked together since the 1990s on County Donegal Railway projects and are the same age.

Also included are some photos, rarely seen, of the dual gauge lines along the quayside at Derry. Where possible we have noted which items of the CDR have survived the more than half a century since closure and where they might be found in 2018.

As for Part One of the Donegal Railway Diary, the photos and text are set out in date order with section headings we created to fit the photographed adventure as well as we thought possible, so still keeping the theme of a diary. The Contents page is assembled accordingly see page 5.

Michael Bunch   Neil Tee   January 2019

Above: Stranorlar goods hauled by Alice leaves Strabane with a consist as described in the text below. Out of sight on the left at the rear of the train is Brake Coach 28 which still survives at Donegal Town.

Donegal Diary Part Two

This is the second part of the diary compiled from both Michael Bunch's own notes and the transcripts of the letters he wrote to life-long colleague David Hyson. While Michael was based in Derry during the 1950s it was fortunate that he described his visits to the then open Donegal Railway in these letters which were equally fortunately kept by David. With this book and its first part an actual experience of the Donegal Railway in print comes to fruition for readers to enjoy.

GOODS TRAINS AT STRABANE

Saturday 28th. January 1956

I caught the 1335 GNR train from Derry to Strabane, arriving there soon after 2pm, just in time to see the Goods leaving for Stranorlar at 1410. I got a picture of it from the station approach road. I also decided that it was about time that I recorded the train formations, and in the following notes, the letter in brackets after a van number, indicates whether it had hinged or sliding doors, or was a convertible type. The train comprised Loco 1 *Alice*, and the following stock:- Ex coach chassis 42, and 45, and vans 191(S), 27(C) , 67(S), 210(C), 288(C), 289(C) 19(H), 257(H), 179(S) 47(S), truck 168, van 50(S) and brake compo 28.

[Key to van type: S=Sliding Doors; C=Convertible Cattle type; H=Hinged Doors.]

Then I walked along the road towards Lifford and waited for the goods from Letterkenny to appear. It came round the long curve from Lifford at 1432, and comprised Loco 2 *Blanche* and vans 197(S), 275(H), 69(S), 65(S), 7(C), Transit truck 44, another truck of unknown number, vans 261(H), 272(H), 2 more trucks unidentified, 6-wheel truck 314, bogie truck 159, truck 300, van 195(S), and brake compo 53.

Then at 1442, Railbus 15 and Red Van 21 departed for Stranorlar, and Railbus 19 with Red Van's 11 & 17 left for Letterkenny. Loco 2 then did a lot of shunting its stock around the yard, and formed its new train, which it propelled up the remains of the Derry branch, and then forward into the Letterkenny line loop for later.

At 1534, Railbus 16 and Red Vans 13 & 10 came in from Stranorlar, and at 1553 Railbus 20, and Red Van 12 arrived from Letterkenny. I set off again towards Lifford, as at 1556 loco 2 and its short train comprising van 2(C), 74(S), Red Van 10, trucks 143, 167 and brake compo 23, went round and over the border bridge to Lifford, reaching there at 1600. It then shunted Van 2 into the bay platform, and Red Van 10 to the Post Office siding. Next vans 48(S), 186(S), 278(H), 266(H), bogie van 320, and transit van 251 were added to the train, which then left Lifford at 1623.

Above: The Letterkenny Goods, a good length of train, coming in to Strabane around the curve from Lifford, headed by locomotive no 2, Blanche, and tailed by brake coach no 53.

Below: Brake 3rd coach no 23 with straight sides, seen at the rear of a goods train departing from Lifford after a period shunting there as described in the text. Coach 23 is one of the same batch built by Oldbury as Coach 28 preserved at Donegal Town.

Above: Open Oldbury-built Transhipment truck 44 at Strabane having been brought in as part of the Letterkenny Goods earlier in the afternoon.

Below: Wagons 300, 159, 314 forming part of the Letterkenny Goods as it comes round the curve into Strabane Station. 300 was a Hurst Nelson wagon delivered for the Strabane & Letterkenny line in 1909. 159 was an original bogie flat from Oldbury. The wagon carrying 314 here was the second incarnation of 314, this one being a conversion from 6-wheel coach No 8.

Goods Trains at Strabane

I walked back over the bridge to Strabane in time to see Railbus 20 with Van 197(S), which van had arrived that afternoon from Letterkenny, depart to Stranorlar at 1655. At 1735, Railbus 16 with three Red Vans, Nos 15, 13, and 12 set off for Letterkenny. By now it was time for me to return to Derry on the GNR line.

Above: Locomotive No 2 Blanche departing from Strabane with the Letterkenny Goods on 28th January 1956.
Below: Locomotive No 5 Drumboe with coach 38 and train attached reversing up the old now closed Derry line at Strabane before running into the Letterkenny platform using the left hand track with this mixed train for Letterkenny on 15th February 1956.

MORE ACTION AT STRABANE & STEAM TO LETTERKENNY

Wednesday 15th. February 1956.

I managed to get an afternoon off today, and so made my way to Strabane, arriving there at approx. 14.05. Soon at 14.17 the goods came in from Stranorlar, comprising Loco 6, and Vans 88(S), 273(H), 54(S), 95(S), 177(S), 191(S), 189(S), 320 Bogie, 202(C), 265(H), and brake compo 28.

The loco ran round the train, and shunted the vans up to the tranship sidings. At 14.20 I could hear the Letterkenny goods arriving at Lifford, and it left there again at 14.42. At 14.44 Railbus 12, with mailvan 15, departed for Stranorlar, just as Loco 5 and train were rounding the bend into Strabane, comprising Vans 240(C), 38(H), 261(H), 83(S), 204(C), 35(C), 201(C), 62(S), 272(H), 53(S), 21(H), 173(S), 283(H), 37(C), 317 Bogie, and trucks 136, 120, and completed with brake compo 53.

Railbus 18, with mailvans 10 and 11, was waiting at the Letterkenny line platform, and departed a couple of minutes later. At 15.30 Railbus 16 with Van 289(C), and Mailvan 22, arrived from Stranorlar. Next arrival was from Letterkenny and this was Railbus 14, and Mailvan 17, at 15.51, and as soon as this had cleared the headshunt, (the old Derry line), Loco 5 propelled its' train up there, and then back down into the Letterkenny platform. At this time the train was timetabled as a mixed train, so it had to use the platform line, and therefore had to wait till after the railbus had come in, instead of using the loop.

The train comprised Coach 38, and Van 11(C), Trucks 311, and 116, Vans 23(C), 246(C), 271(H), 241(C), 68(S), 281(H), 75(S), 63(S), 284(H), 294(C), 179(S), 181(S), and Brake compo 23. This was a heavy train for a Class 5 loco. I boarded coach 38, and we departed at 16.01, reaching Lifford at 16.04.

Here we stayed while the Customs did a protracted check of the whole train, plus a little shunting, so that we did not depart from there till 17.17. We reached Raphoe at 17.41, and we were told that as we were so late myself and a handful of other passengers should transfer to the closely following Railbus to continue our journey to Letterkenny.

This was a disappointment to me as I had made the special effort to get the time off for the express purpose of the doing the whole line behind steam. So I decided that rather than waste the money, by returning to Strabane on the railbus that we were crossing, I would complete the journey, and experience the line in the dark.

I returned from Letterkenny on the same railbus, and reached Raphoe at 19.40. Loco 5 and its train were still in the loop waiting to continue their journey, now minus coach 38, which was left in the siding at Raphoe. On arrival at Strabane, I was able to get the GNR back to Derry.

Below: Diesel tractor Phœnix with Coach 38 and wagons shunting in the transhipment area at Strabane.

Above: The interior of Coach 38 (non-window end) showing seating and the shadow under the end seat is the heater unit.
Below: View from Coach 38 towards the back of the heavy Letterkenny mixed train as it left Strabane.

Above: Trailer 6 in the sidings at Strabane. This side view shows clearly how it was modified in 1945 from Railcar 6, the bonnet and engine section having been removed from the left leaving the sloping windscreen. On the right hand side the curved rear panels of the original railcar were still used for the trailer.
Below: On the same day at Strabane this is Coach No 28 at the rear of the departing goods to Stranorlar. Coach 28, originally from Oldbury in 1893, is preserved at Donegal Town.

A BUSY AFTERNOON OF ACTIVITY AT STRABANE

Saturday 19th. May 1956.

I had my first visit to Strabane today for some time, owing to other commitments. I arrived at 14.05, just in time to see Railbuses 12 and 10 with vans 257(H), and 76(S), coming in from Stranorlar. After the passengers alighted, the railbuses moved on to the sidings, and No 10 retired to the engine shed.

At 14.08, Loco 1 came round from Lifford with only one van, No. 207(C), having left the rest of the goods train at Lifford, see picture below. It came through the platform line and passed Loco 2 in the loop.

Loco 2 went round to Lifford at 14.11 to pick up the rest of the goods from Letterkenny. Loco 1 left its' van in the sidings, and immediately coupled up to the Stranorlar goods, which comprised Vans 37(C), 201(C), 84(S), 182(S), 270(H), 86(S), and trucks 297, and 213, completed with brake compo 28, and departed at 14.20.

At 14.36, Loco 2 brought the rest of the goods from Lifford, comprising, low bogie flat 336, and Vans 275(H), 15(C), 248(C), 177(S), 280(H), 273(H), and brake compo 53, and came to rest in the Letterkenny line loop. Railbus 20 with coach 40, and mailvans 13, and 15, was positioned in the Letterkenny platform alongside Loco 2's train in the loop..

At 14.46, No 20, with coach 40 ran forward, leaving the mailvans at the platform, and then shunted coach 40 onto the back of the goods. No 20 then returned to the platform and coupled up to the two vans, by 14.48. Meanwhile Railbus 12 with Mailvan 11 departed for Stranorlar at 14.50, and ten minutes later, now some 25 minutes behind schedule, Railbus 20, and vans departed to Letterkenny. The next arrival was from Stranorlar, at 15.33, when Railbus 14, with Trailer 2, Van 59(S) and Mailvan 10, came in. Later at 16.02, Railbus 16, with coach 30, and mailvan 21 arrived from Letterkenny, allowing Loco 2 with the goods for Letterkenny, comprising vans 209(H), 268(H), 326(H), 56(S), 54(S), 198(S), 94(S), 175(S), 38(C), 85(S), 261(H), 203(C), and 4-wheel flat 254, carrying an ancient Austin (for photo see part 1 of the Michael Bunch Donegal Railway Diary page 2), and finally brake compo 23, to leave four minutes later.

Before I left Strabane I noted that Railbus 14, with Trailer 2 was at the Stranorlar platform, and Railbus 16 was at the Letterkenny platform. I presume the swapping of the loco's was because No 1 was due for servicing at Stranorlar.

Below: Loco No 1, Alice, coming round the curve from Lifford into Strabane, see text above

Above: An unusual view of two class 5A locomotives in operation at Strabane. Here, shunting manoeuvres described on page 16 have resulted in No 1 Alice taking water at the Letterkenny platform in Strabane alongside No 2 Blanche which was in the loop ready to continue on to Lifford to collect the rest of the train that No 1 had originally brought from Letterkenny. No 1 had brought just the one goods van (a convertible cattle van) with it and this can be seen on the far left behind the water bag.

Below: Loco No 1 Alice departing Strabane on the Stranorlar Goods on 19th May 1956. Note the healthy consist of the train implying there was still plenty of demand for goods to be taken by train between the two towns. Out of sight on the left was Coach 28 bringing up the rear of the train.

A busy afternoon of activity at Strabane

Above: Loco No 2 Blanche bringing in the Letterkenny train bunker first having gone to fetch it from the customs in Lifford a little earlier as described in the text on page 16. The first bogey wagon is the 40 feet long ex-Ballymena Cushendall and Red Bay Railway flat no 336, once a coach on that line. The 40 foot length was extremely useful for dealing with long loads on the County Donegal lines.
Below: A close-up of flat no 336 showing the end detail and the raised coupling arrangement.

Above: Brake Coach 53 on right with Coach 40 on left in the loop line at the Letterkenny platform at Strabane Station. Coach 53 was one of the brake coaches from Oldbury originally delivered for the Strabane and Letterkenny line in 1907.

Below: A good view of Coach 40 in the Letterkenny platform at Strabane. Built by Pickering in 1905, number 40 became a 60 seater coach after its end access platforms were boxed in.

Above: Loco No 2 Blanche with the Letterkenny Goods leaving Strabane at 16.06 on 19th May 1956 as described in the text on page 16.
Below: Coach 14 in the sidings at Strabane on the same day. One of the batch supplied by Oldbury in 1893, Coach 14 survives to this day in the defunct Foyle Valley Railway museum by the Craigavon Bridge in Derry, now taken over by the Destined group. Note the shunting signal in the foreground.

THE LETTERKENNY LINE

Monday 28th. May 1956

Today, I had arranged to meet Bruce Heaven. He is the man who sells blueprints of Irish narrow gauge stock, and I have had several drawings from him. He is staying a few days in the area, and we are going .to meet at Strabane. I was able to get there at 09.05 by catching a bus from Derry at 8am. He with his wife turned up soon after, and we made ourselves known to each other, as we had never previously met. We were able to watch the comings and goings for a while, which included Railbus 10 with Trailer 2 and mailvan 20 arriving from Stranorlar at 09.29, see picture below.

The trailer and van were left in the sidings while No 10 turned and returned to the platform now with Van 239(C), ready for its' next duty. Looking across to Lifford we could see Railbus 12 with mailvan 22, arrive there at 09.40. It stopped for ten minutes, and arrived at Strabane at 09.52. At 10.00 Railbus 10 and van departed for Stranorlar. After a lull, Phœnix and van 202(C) ran round to Lifford at 1037. At 10.55 Railbus 20 with Vans 56(S) and 278(H) came in from Stranorlar.

A minute later, Phœnix came back from Lifford with Vans 55(S) and 202(C). After a while the two Railbuses, having been turned on the turntable, came back to their respective platforms, No 20 with mailvans 11 and 14. No. 12 also had two vans. We boarded No 12 for Letterkenny, and both railbuses pulled out simultaneously at 11.26. As I had travelled this line recently on the steam train, I could remember where most of the ¼ mile posts were, and sat near the front so I could sight them through the front window of this half cab railbus. We reached Lifford in less than two minutes. One van was left here, and we continued on our way just after 11.43. Along the level I estimated we got up to 36mph and reached Ballindrait at 11.48. We stopped there for less than two minutes, and went on to Raphoe, not stopping at Coolaghy. On the banks up to Raphoe we slowed to less than 19mph, at around 5 ¼ miles.

We reached there at exactly 12.00, paused for one minute, and passed Railbus 19 in the loop, reaching Convoy in just over 7 minutes. We stopped there for nearly three minutes, and then ran the rest of the way to Letterkenny non-stop, reaching there at 12.34. I estimated our total running time was 47 minutes. We had nearly 2 hours to wait at Letterkenny, and we saw Loco 2 and its train depart before going to have a meal, then returning on the same Railbus, again with one van. We left at 14.39, and reached Strabane at 15.53, with an actual running time of 54 minutes.

As at this time the afternoon goods to Letterkenny was still running as a mixed train, we had to wait till No 12 was clear of the head shunt before coming to the Letterkenny line platform. It comprised Loco 2, with Coach 40 and vans 47(S), and 275(H) with bogie truck 334, and 4-wheel flat 254 and Brake Coach 23.

Now we had some time to wait, so we went and measured coaches 58 and 59 which were in the sidings at the south end. Then Bruce and his wife bade farewell and went on Railbus 16, with Van 71(S) to Donegal where they were to spend the night departing at 16.46. Meanwhile as I left, I saw Railbus 12 with mailvans 10, and 20 waiting at the Letterkenny platform.

Below: Railcar No 10 towing Trailer 2 and Red Van 20 from Stranorlar across the bridge over the Mourne into Strabane, see text above.

Above: A goods train with a healthy consist departing from Letterkenny Station on 28th May 1956, with loco No 2 Blanche hauling it bunker first, and brake coach 53 bringing up the rear. Coach 53 was one of a group supplied by Oldbury in 1907 for the opening of the Strabane and Letterkenny line and lasted until the end of the railway.
Below: Loco 2 Blanche bringing the afternoon mixed train for Letterkenny into the Letterkenny platform at Strabane having had to wait for the incoming Railcar 12 from Letterkenny, on which the photographer travelled, to clear the headshunt as described on page 21.

REMAINING COACHES

June 1956

I wrote again to the CDR, and received in reply a list of all the coaches still in use, giving me seating capacity, name of builder, and date of build. There were now only 21 coaches left in use.

I also enquired as to the fate of the older 6-wheel coaches, and was told that Coaches 5, 7 and 9 had been converted into open trucks. The letter was actually signed by Mr B L Curran, then manager of the CDRJC.

A BRIDGE DISAPPEARS

Friday 15th. June 1956

I read in a local paper during the week that the bridge of the former CDR line over the main Londonderry to Strabane road a mile out of Derry had been removed to make way for road improvements. This evening as it was nice I walked along to the site of Bridge 630, to get a picture.

Above: The site of bridge 630 looking north on the approach to Derry. The River Foyle is out of sight to the left. The bridge before demolition appears on page 59 of Part 1.
Below: Loco No 6 Columbkille with Coach 53 during preparation of the goods for Stranorlar that afternoon.

GOODS & PASSENGER TRAINS TO & FROM STRABANE

Wednesday 7th. August 1956.

I had an afternoon off today, so made my way down to Strabane, arriving there at 14.15. I was in time to see both the afternoon goods trains depart. First was at 1440 when Loco 6 with Vans 29(C), 206(C), 326(H), 35(C), 272(H), 190(S), 256(H), 259(H), 48(S), 47(S), 261(H), Trucks 228, 143, and brake compo 53 was going to Stranorlar.

Above: Loco 4 Meenglas preparing the Letterkenny goods in the loop on the Letterkenny platform at Strabane. The final consist is given in the text on this page.
Below: Railcar 19 at the Letterkenny platform in Strabane awaiting to connect to Coach 15 which was conveying a party of scouts.

Five minutes later, Loco 4 with Vans 94(S), 71(S), Tranship van 251, 283(H), 285(C), 208(C), 255(H), 247(C), 281(H), 270(H), Truck 140, Flat 254, Bogie flat 319, and brake compo 23, left for Letterkenny. Then at the two platforms the Railbuses were positioned for their next workings.

At the Letterkenny platform was Railbus 19 with coach 15, filled with a party of boy scouts, and Mailvans 12 and 16. That left at 14.51, and at the Stranorlar platform, was Railbus 14, with Trailer 3, and Mailvans 15 and 20. I boarded Trailer 3, and we left at 14.58. We arrived at Castlefinn at 15.11, and we crossed Railbus 12 with coach 30, Trailer 5, and mailvans 11 and 19, and overtook the goods train which was in the siding. We left Castlefinn at 15.20, and with brief stops at Killygordon and Liscooly, We arrived at Stranorlar at 15.39.

Railbus 14 left its load at Stranorlar, and continued on to Donegal solo at 15.45. At 16.25, the goods train arrived from Castlefinn, and moved into the sidings. I sought permission to have a look around the sidings, and found Coaches 39 and 43, awaiting scrapping. At 17.48 Railbus 12 with Van 94(S) returned from Strabane, and ran right up onto the remaining stub of the Glenties branch, clear of the mainline. Then at 18.00, Railbus 20 with van 257(H), and mailvan 14, came in from Donegal, and stopped at the far end of the platform, so that No 12, could back out from its' siding onto the platform, and then set off for Donegal at 18.04. I boarded No 20 for my return to Strabane, and left at 18.08. Reached Castlefinn at 18.28, and passed Railbus 16, with Trailer 5, and towing Railbus 10 backwards. Then Railbus 20 shunted van 257 into the sidings and picked up Mailvan 14, before continuing on to Strabane at 18.37, arriving there at 19.03. I then returned to Derry.

Above: On 7th August 1956 here are, from left, coaches 58, 59 & 57 in the sidings near the Camel's Hump at Strabane, presumably awaiting their use for the next excursion, though Coach 58 was often used as a railcar trailer.

Below: Coach 57 in the sidings at Strabane. Like its luxury sister coaches numbers 58 & 59, this came to the CDR from the NCC lines when they closed in 1950.

Above: The carriage sidings at Stranorlar looking north with coaches, from left, 28, 16, 32, 46, 33, 12 and 40. Coach 28 was an 1893 Oldbury example with straight sides, and it survives on display at Donegal Town in 2018.
Bottom: Coach 43 in the scrap siding at Stranorlar on 7th August 1956 with coach 39 beyond. Both were supplied by Pickering in 1905.

DOWN TO STRANORLAR

Saturday 18th August 1956

I had a visit to the CDR today, with my fiancé, so was not able to take many notes. I did see that the following coaches were in the sidings at the south end of Strabane:- 13, 14, 17, 53, 57, 58, and 59. Coach 28 was on the Goods which came in from Letterkenny. Railbus 12 with coach 40 (see photo on the right) was at the Letterkenny platform, and we boarded Railbus 14 that was towing Trailer 5, plus a mailvan, to go to Stranorlar.

At Castlefinn we passed both the passenger and goods trains. At the platform were Railbuses 19 and 20 hauling coaches 15 and 12, with Trailer 3, van 259(H) and mailvan 17. In the siding was Loco 5 and its train with brake compo coach 23. At Stranorlar there were a further five coaches in the bay platform. Before we left, I did ascertain that there was to be a Hills of Donegal excursion the next day, in conjunction with the GNR from Derry. My fiancé and I then caught a bus back to Derry.

LOTS OF ACTION AT STRABANE

Sunday 19th. August 1956.

I caught a bus down to Strabane, arriving there at about 10.00. There were now ten coaches in the sidings this morning. These three sidings originally served the cattle dock, and a small goods shed, but since the demise of cattle trains, they were used for storing carriages to be used on Sunday excursions. I have numbered the sidings 1 to 3 from east to west. Siding 1 being that nearest to the cattle dock. In this siding were coaches 12, and 13. In siding 2 were 53, and 58, while in the outer siding, No. 3 were 30, 15, 17, 14, 59, and 57. Coach 40, and Railbuses 12, 16, and 20 were also present by the engine shed. .

At 10.20, Railbus 20, towing No. 16 ran into the Stranorlar loop line. No. 20 uncoupled and ran into siding 3. Coach 30 was shunted from siding 3 to siding 1. At 10.25, Railbus 20 pulled out coaches 15, 17, and 14 from siding 3, and then shunted coach 14 into siding 1. By 10.27 coach 17 was put back into siding 3. Finally Railbus 20, with coach 15 went to siding 1 and stopped. Railbus 16 retired to the sheds.

At 10.47, Railbus 19, towing No. 18 backwards approach from Stranorlar, and ran into the Stranorlar platform. Then at 10.50 Railbus 20, pulls out coaches 15, 14, and 30 from siding 1 and runs into the loop line. Railbus 18, starts up and runs towards Stranorlar, and then backs on to the three coaches. No 19 goes on to the sheds.

By this time the GNR train is on its' way from Derry so presumably it is known how many passengers will be using the excursion. At 10.52, Railbus 18 with only coach 30 pulls out on to the mainline, and then backs in to the Stranorlar platform.

No 20 then pushed coaches 14, and 15 back in to siding 1. Railbus 20 then shunts backwards and forwards, to position itself at the head of No. 18 and coach 30 at the platform. At about 11.00, the GNR train arrived, headed by Loco 106, and eight coaches. 126 passengers detrained and crossed over to the CDR platform, in the customary way, of walking round in front of the Loco. At 11.20 Railbuses 20, 18 and coach 30 depart on their way to Ballyshannon. The GNR train would also go there by its' route via Omagh. Later, I think about 13.30 Railbus 19 with coach 40 departed to Stranorlar. The extra Railbuses and coaches presumably being available if required, as this excursion has been made up to four railbuses, three coaches and a 4-wheel Trailer if there was enough demand.

Lots of action at Strabane

Above: Railcar No16 in the loop line at the Stranorlar platform in Strabane Station as part of the shunting operations described on page 29.

Below: Railcar No 19 towing Railcar No 18 empty stock from Stranorlar to Strabane almost ready to arrive at Strabane as it passes over the Mourne Bridge. This shows that there was in fact a prototype for seeing the railcars in use back to back. This later happened with Railcars 19 & 20 on the Isle of Man and with Railcars 18 & 12 in the late 1990s on the 3-foot gauge track laid to the south of the Foyle Valley Museum in Derry.

Above: Railcar 20 shunting coaches 15, 17 and 14 at the south end of Strabane Station on Sunday 19th August 1956 as part of the preparations for a Hills of Donegal Excursion, proving that these were not always steam-hauled but sometimes consisted of "teams" of railcars, trailers and coaches. Coach 14 survives in the closed Foyle Valley Museum in Derry.

Below: Railcar 20 coupled to Railcar 18 hauling saloon coach 30 with end windows forming the 11.20 Hills of Donegal Excursion leaving Strabane for Ballyshannon. on the same day as the above picture.

Above: Coaches 15, 14 & 12 in the southern sidings at Strabane alongside the Camel's Hump. All these coaches were supplied by Oldbury in 1893 and survived to the end of the railway. Numbers 12 & 15 were part of the abortive Dr Cox purchase but No 14 could be seen in the Foyle Valley Museum in Derry until its closure.
Below: Coach 12 in centre, with coach 14 to left and coach 17 to right. Number 17 was, like Number 15, part of the Dr Cox purchase and this coach survived to the end of services. Note the canopy of the goods shed which stood on the same siding as the cattle pens.

Above: A close-up of Coach 14, which survives to this day, here seen under the canopy of the goods shed in the southern sidings at Strabane Station.
Below: Coach 57 with Coach 59 beyond and the slightly shorter Coach 58 to the right. The traces of the original corridor connections on these ex-NCC coaches can be clearly seen.

STRABANE, STRANORLAR & LIFFORD ACTIVITY

Saturday 22nd September 1956

I went to Strabane today, on one of the new GNR diesel sets, No's 612 and 613. As this is the Belfast Express, it included a breakfast car between the power cars. We left Derry at 09.37, and reached Strabane in about 20 minutes.

At 10.00, Railbus 10 with three vans and one truck departed to Stranorlar. At 10.40 Phœnix took Vans 12(H), 260(H), Tranship van 251, and truck 167 to Lifford.

At 10.50, Railbus 16 with mailvan 21, Vans 241(C) and 294(C), arrived from Stranorlar. At 11.05 Phœnix returned from Lifford with vans 256(H), 260, and 12 again.

Then Railbus 18 moved onto the Letterkenny line with mailvan 14, and Railbus 16 with Mailvan 21, came to the Stranorlar platform. I boarded No 16, to go to Donegal. No 18 departed at 11.21, and we left a minute later.

Above: Railcar 10 leaving Strabane at 10 am with three vans and a wagon, see text above. This must have been near to the maximum permitted load for No 10.
Below: Looking from the GNR platform to the narrow gauge Stranorlar platform at Strabane. Note the change in gauge as you scan the photo left to right. The Letterkenny platform is on the other side of the building. Note the customs tables and barrier on the CDR's Strabane platform.

We reached Castlefinn at 11.45. Here we passed Loco 11 with coach 14, which I was told had brought passengers all the way from Killybegs, and several vans with brake compo 28 at the rear. We left Castlefinn at 11.50 and reached Stranorlar at 12.14. We only stopped for three minutes here and went on to Doncgal arriving at 13.07.

I had a quick lunch there and returned in Railbus 19 with mailvan 15, departing at 14.20. We arrived at Stranorlar at 15.15. Here we backed onto Trailer 3 and mailvan 13 which were in the Glenties spur, and also were passed by Railbus 20 with Trailer 5. We set off again at 13.25, and reached Castlefinn at 15.50, arriving at Strabane at 16.10 (below).

Above: Railcar 19, Trailer 3 and two vans on the 13.25 from Stranorlar having arrived at Strabane at 16.10 on Saturday 22nd September 1956.

Below: Looking north from the GNR side at Strabane showing rolling stock in the GNR sidings at centre right and the narrow gauge sidings in centre with Trailer 3 in front of the sheds. The old narrow gauge Derry line, by now closed, was beyond the left edge of the narrow gauge platform, left of the tall signal.

At Castlefinn we again passed Loco 11, with coach 40, several vans and brake compo 28, and arrived back at Strabane at 16.10. This was just in time to see Loco 2 with a heavy train of 22 vans and brake compo 23 depart for Letterkenny at 16.13, see bottom picture on this page.

Above: Coach 40 resting outside the goods shed at the southern sidings in Strabane after being brought by a mixed train hauled by Loco 11, Erne, as described in the text.
Below: A heavy afternoon goods train leaving Strabane for Letterkenny containing 22 vans and brake coach 23. The train was hauled by Loco No 2, Blanche, just out of sight on right.

MORE STRABANE, STRANORLAR & LIFFORD ACTIVITY

Saturday 6th October 1956

I went down to Strabane by bus today so as to arrive a bit earlier. At 12.54, Loco 4 with coach 14, Vans 10(C), 46(S), 208(C), 279(H), 71(S), 271(H), 288(C), 205(C), 26(C), 285(C), 284(H), 89(S), 69(S), 68(S) plus wagons 130, 295, 230, 297, 167, and brake compo 28 arrived from Stranorlar, timetabled as a mixed train, and stopped at the platform. A few passengers alighted including Inspector McBride.

Simultaneously, Loco 2 was shunting on the Stranorlar line loop, and I got a picture of the two loco's sided by side. At 13.15, Phoenix set off for Lifford, with eight vans, and returned at 13.50 with vans 61(S), 21(H), 274(H), 7(C), and mailvan 22.

At 14.04 Railbus 15, with vans 3(C), and 55(S), departed to Stranorlar, and only eleven minutes later, Loco 4, with coach 14, nine vans and brake compo 28, followed to Stranorlar. The eleven minutes being the time it took the railbus to get to Clady.

At 14.28, Loco No 5, Drumboe, with coach 32, and van 286(C), came round from Lifford. The loco uncoupled and ran round its short train and headed off back to Lifford. Loco No 2, Blanche, then came and moved the coach and van into the sidings. At 14.44 Railbus 15, Van27(C), and mailvan 10 departed to Stranorlar. At 14.56 Loco No 5 returned from Lifford with the rest of the goods comprising Vans 37(C), 2(C), 60(S), Truck 121, Vans 280(H), 179(S), 53(S), 247(C), 91(S), 173(S), 31(C), Tranship van 155, 263(H), 289(C), 178(S), Bogie van 333, and brake compo 23.

Immediately Railbus 16, with mailvans 18 and 17 departed to Letterkenny. Now there was a lull of nearly an hour, before Railbus 14, with coach 40 and mailvan 16 arrived from Letterkenny at 15.55. Meanwhile Loco No 5 with vans 3(C), 286(C), 326(H), 177(S), 75(S), Truck 167, Bogie truck 159, Truck 311, Bogie van 319, Low bogie flat 336 and brake compo 53 were waiting to depart, doing so five minutes later.

Finally before I left, Railbus 12 with Trailer 3, mailvans 21, and 13, arrived from Stranorlar at 16.12. Note there were 3 loco's in steam today. This is my last visit to the railway, as I am leaving the airforce in a few days. However I will be able to keep up with events with the local newspapers which will be sent to me in England.

Below: Loco No 4 Meenglas having just arrived at Strabane with a long mixed train from Stranorlar on Saturday 6th October 1956. The consist is described in the text above. Inspector McBride was travelling on the train and can be seen in the raincoat just to the right of the signal post.

Above: Locos No 2, Blanche, (left), and No 4, Meenglas, side by side on the Stranorlar side of Strabane Station on 6th October 1956. Meenglas had just arrived with the mixed train from Stranorlar and Blanche was shunting.
Below: No 5, Drumboe, with coach 32 and van 286 having just arrived at Strabane from Lifford.

Above: Loco No 5 Drumboe shunting Coach 32 in the Letterkenny loop at Strabane.
Below: Loco No 4 Meenglas on a long mixed train departing Strabane for Stranorlar.

Above: Railcar 10 with goods van in the main platform at Stranorlar with a train for Strabane. The decorative nature of the roofing and upright columns is clear as is the characterful nature of the main station building with its tower. Railcar 10 survives complete at Cultra but the lovely station buildings were demolished, one of the more inexcusable removals of railway heritage. Photo by David Hyson.

Below: A view looking towards Donegal (and, originally to the right, Glenties) along the main platform at Stranorlar. Visible are the stanchions holding up the canopy to the right, the footbridge at centre right, then the general stores building and on left the carriage and wagon repair shop. None of this exists now, the only link with transport being the CIE buses that park on the concrete that covers the railway formation. Photo by David Hyson.

Above: Loco No 4 Meenglas with the three ex-NCC luxury coaches at Stranorlar. The coaches are, from right to left, Nos 58, 57 & 59. No 58 was significantly shorter than the others as can be seen in the photo. No 58's body can still be seen at Donegal Town Station over 60 years after this photo.

Below: In the text we are told how the driver may have tried just a little harder than usual knowing that there were some enthusiasts on the train and this is the view that Michael and David would have seen of the trucks "jumping up and down on the track" as they swung up the Finn Valley between Stranorlar and Strabane. Photo by David Hyson.

Above: A view back from the brake coach of the train between Stranorlar and Strabane, probably at Killygordon Station, where the road overbridge that can be seen in the distance still exists, as does the main station building. Photo by David Hyson.

Below: A half-cab railcar (probably 14) facing the photographer in the down platform and the long freight on which he travelled fast from Stranorlar in the up platform at Castlefinn. Note the platforms are signalled for both directions. Photo by David Hyson.

Above left: Loco No 11, Erne, the last suriving Baltic tank on Irish railways at Strabane on Tuesday 23rd April 1957. Built in 1904 by Nasmyth Wilson, Erne lasted until the end of the CDR, and was part of the Dr Cox purchases for preservation. Sadly this never happened and Erne was scrapped, apparently without authority, after lying derelict at Letterkenny until around 1967. Photo by David Hyson.
Above right: A close-up of the motion of Erne for modellers. Photo by David Hyson.
Below: Erne's driver doing a pre-journey inspection at Strabane This picture also shows Erne from a different angle than the other two photos on this page. Photo by David Hyson.

Above: Railcar 12, Trailer 2 and a red van on the Stranorlar Platform at Strabane preparing a train for Stranorlar. Note the customs fence and table on the platform, a source of many delays in the 1950s that could recur at the border between Northern Ireland and the Republic with the advent of Brexit. Photo by David Hyson.
Below: Railcar 18 and Trailer 3 at Strabane having arrived with a train. Photo by David Hyson.

Above: Railcar 18 and red van at Strabane on the platform for Stranorlar. The picture is taken looking across the Great Northern Railway broad gauge platform. Photo by David Hyson.

Below: Coach 32 and others in the southern sidings at Strabane alongside the main line to Stranorlar which is the track nearest the photographer. Note the substantial footbridge in the background.

Above: Near Raphoe, a view of the track taken from the brake coach of the goods train to Letterkenny.
Below: The remains of the harbour branch at Letterkenny south of the station. This was accessed by the CDR although right here the Swilly line was adjacent as they crossed the Swilly river. The buildings on the left and the remains of the gate lasted into the 2000s, and a mural of the train was even painted onto one of the houses but these are now demolished and all of this has disappeared. The picture is a little blurred due to the movement of the train but records of this spot are rare.

CHANGE OF USE AT VICTORIA ROAD

July 1957

I have just read in the Belfast Telegraph, that a firm of wholesale grocers, Messrs O'Neill and McHenry, have acquired the old station buildings at Victoria Road. The railway premises will have to be adapted for our use, said Mr Towers, Director of the firm.

BUSY DECEMBER ON THE CDR

Thursday 19th December 1957

I am back in Ireland and spending Christmas with my in-laws. I was able to come to Strabane today, arriving at 10.30. Phoenix was doing its' usual bit of shunting, and I noted coaches 17 and 30, in the sidings. I boarded Railbus 18, with mailvans 12 and 11, on what should have been the 11.35 departure to Stranorlar, but we actually left at 12.07.

Above: A view of the closed CDR station at Derry from the Craigavon Bridge.
Below: Railcar 18 with red vans 12 & 11 waiting to leave Strabane a little late on Thursday 19th December 1957. Railcar 18 survives on the Fintown Railway at Fintown in 2018.

Busy December on the CDR

At Castlefinn, we passed Loco 5 and mixed train, including coaches 14, 15, 16, and 56, and reached Stranorlar at 12.50.

I browsed around the sidings there, and found coach chassis Nos 33, 34, 39, 46, 50, 51, and 52, of which 33 & 46, had only recently had their bodies removed. There was a big pile of doors still on the ground.

I found somewhere to have lunch at Ballybofey, then caught the 15.15 back to Strabane, again passing the goods at Castlefinn. I arrived at Strabane in time to see the recently repaired Loco No 2, Blanche, departing on the Letterkenny goods. I noted that the following stock had been repainted this year - Loco No 2, Trailer 3, Railbus 20, and coach 30 in October and coach 56 in August 1957.

Above: What must have been a fairly typical scene at Stranorlar in the last years of the railway. Here we see the chassis of Coach 46. Behind are vans 292 and 49.

Below: The doors saved after the scrapping of coaches 43 and 46 in the yard at Stranorlar. This enabled the continuation of the "make do and mend" policy that had been in place on the railway for years.

Two views of Railcar Trailer 3 spotted at Stranorlar on 19th December 1957
Above: Trailer 3 standing on the small turntable at the western end of the Station beside the stub end of the old branch to Glenties. In this view the signal box can be seen behind the railcar while underneath the railcar can be seen part of the unusual wheel arrangement, effectively a 2-2-2-2 with the outer two pairs of wheels smaller than the other four. Also visible is the curved panel at one end and a doorway at the other.
Below: Trailer 3 from the other side showing the symmetry. It was sourced second-hand from the broad gauge Dublin and Blessington Steam Tramway in 1934 and ran with an engine on the CDR until 1944 after which is was converted to a trailer and lasted until the end of services in 1959. It was saved for preservation and can be seen in the museum in Cultra.

Above: Coach 32 built by Oldbury in 1901 seen here at Stranorlar. Coach 32 survived to the end of the railway to be auctioned off in 1961.

Below: Coach 17 at Strabane from a batch built by Oldbury in 1893, though unlike its sister coaches this one and number 16 had beaded panelling unlike the matchboarding of the 1893 brake coach 28 which is a survivor. Coach 17 lasted to the end of the railway to be part of the abortive Dr Cox purchase ending in dereliction and destruction at Strabane.

Above: Grey vans 19 & 17 at Strabane. They differ in that No 17 on the right can be seen to be a convertible cattle van, with the shutters that could be slid down to the stops at waist level of the van to provide ventilation for the animals. No 19 was a simple hinged-door goods van.

Below: 4 days later, and two days before Christmas 1957, plenty of steam up at Strabane with a Class 5A No 2 Blanche in the middle, and two Class 5 locos No 5 Drumboe and No 6 Columbkille. What a great scene that is now covered by the metal sculpture The Tinnies.

Above: Coach 56 in the southern sidings at Strabane Station. One of the 1907 batch from Oldbury originally supplied for the Strabane and Letterkenny line, it was then a composite with six compartments laid out 3,2,1,1,2,3 the compartment size differences being identifiable from the distances between the windows on the coach side. The coach lasted to the end of services and in its last years was converted to an all third.
Below: A rather shabby looking coach 16 in the southern sidings at Strabane. This was the twin of Coach 17 shown on page 60, and like its twin it lasted until the end of the railway and was part of the abortive Dr Cox purchase.

Christmas on the CDR

Above: Railcar 19, Railcar 12 and Coach 30 at the Letterkenny platform in Strabane ready to leave for Letterkenny on 23rd December 1957 as described on page 62. Two red mail vans have yet to be added to the train, making it quite a mixed consist.

Below: A rare sight of three CDR locos in steam and on shunting duties in the southern sidings at Strabane Station. The locos are Class 5 numbers 5 & 6 and Class 5A no 2. There appears to be no-one on the Camel's Hump bridge on the right but it would have been quite a scene to look at.

we reached our Ballyshannon destination, at 14.18 hrs, after just over three hours travelling.

I took photographs at Ballyshannon, and had time to visit the GNR station which had closed earlier that year, before returning to catch the 16.00 hrs departure back to Donegal Town. This left 5 mins late with vans 271 and 279 in tow This part of the journey was equally slow, and the railcar was full of school-girls, on their way home. As we passed the big Church, up on the hill at Rossnowlagh, they all dutifully crossed themselves. There were several other brief stops.

At Donegal Town I had only eight minutes to wait for Railcar 14 to come in from Killybegs. This was towing

vans 37 and 119, which were parked in a siding and then coupled up Mail vans 14, and 15, and we left Donegal five mins late at 17.13. Passing Lough Eske, I saw that Railcar 18 was being attended to in the siding, and we waited to pass Loco 5 and its train, Van 277(H), an unidentifiable bogie flat, Vans 281(H), 66(S), 12(H), 288(C), 78(S), and brake compo 23. Once clear of Lough Eske we ascended up into the Barnesmore at a fair speed, not stopping at any of the halts, and reached Stranorlar at 18.03 again just five minutes late. Although there was nothing to pass there, we stayed for nearly six minutes, before leaving for Strabane four minutes late.

Above: Ballyshannon Station looking south on 2nd September 1958, with a significant number of goods vehicles in the sidings. The station master's house still stands though extended.
Below: Ballyshannon Station looking north on the same day from the platform. On the left is the unusual goods shed with triple canopy shelters and a goods van during the loading/unloading process. The goods shed has disappeared completely. Over to the right behind the signal is Trailer 2 which survived to the end of the railway in 1959. The base of the water tower behind Trailer 2 still exists.

Above: A close-up view of Trailer 2 at Ballyshannon. This began life as a railcar on the Castlederg and Victoria Bridge Tramway. It was bought without an engine by Henry Forbes for the CDR and for a while ran with a Reo engine, then being converted in 1944 to a trailer with 30 seats, almost double that of its railcar existence.

Below: A somewhat blurred picture of Railcar 14 due to its movement as it arrives under the Donegal Town footbridge from Killybegs on 2nd September 1958 towing a convertible cattle van. Note the significantly curved tops to the windows by which Railcar 14 could be identified.

A visit to Glenties

Above: A fuller view of the engine shed and the water tower from the approach road to Glenties Station. The turntable was just to the right of the water tower, hence the need for the chamfer of the corner brickwork when the longer railcars started visiting Glenties in the 1930s. There was also a carriage shed to the left of the engine shed but this was of corrigated iron and steel uprights and so was suffering from rust and neglect. Photo by Neil Tee.
Below: A view of Glenties as if from a train approaching from Stranorlar. The goods shed, which was demolished in the early 2000s, is on the left and in the undergrowth on the photographer's side of the shed the cattle dock could still be detected as late as 2003. The station building is in the centre. Behind the photographer was originally a level crossing over the main road. Photo by Neil Tee.

PROGRESS AT VICTORIA ROAD, DERRY

Friday 8th September 1958

I was in Derry this afternoon, and took a few pictures along the quay side of the mixed gauge tracks (see also pages 105-109). The three foot gauge tracks were long disused, but still some activity on the 5' 3" lines used by the GNR. Also had a look at the work taking place at Victoria Road Station. All of the platform area under the overall roof is being boxed in.

Below: Progress on the boxing in of Victoria Road Station in Derry while the original station roof and its attractive wrought iron uprights is being retained. The Craigavon Bridge is in the background.

Bottom: A picture of the station interior resulting from the boxing in some 45 years later in 2003 when the station was occupied by a bathroom sales organisation. Note how the attractive wrought ironwork was indeed retained. Photo by Neil Tee.

ACTIVITY AT STRABANE

Saturday 9th September 1958

I arrived at Strabane at 13.30, and noted that Railbus 12 was just in from Stranorlar, and No 18 from Letterkenny. Loco 5 was shunting, and Loco 4 was at the sheds. Coaches 23, 30, 56, and 58, were in the sidings. At 13.45, Phœnix came round from Lifford with Mailvan 21. Later Phœnix added coach 58 to the back of Railbus 12 which was standing at the Stranorlar platform. I note that coach 58 is now used as a Railbus trailer, and has its' lights connected to the Railbus supply.

At 14.29, Railbus 12 with coach 58 and Mailvan 11 left for Stranorlar. Railbus 18 with Mailvans 16 and 13 moved to the Letterkenny platform to await the arrival of the goods from Letterkenny. This duly arrived at 14.43, and comprised Loco 2 with Van 86(S), Tranship van 253, Van 92, Tranship van 251, Truck 121, Vans 61(S), 175(S), 294(C), Coach chassis 48, Vans 8(C), 52(S), 255(H), 210(C), 264(H), and Brake compo 53. Six minutes later the Railbus departed, some 14 minutes late.

Above: Phœnix (just visible on the left) bringing Coach 58 from the sidings at Strabane to attach to the train for Stranorlar to be hauled by Railcar 12.
Below: Railcar 12 with Coach 58 as a trailer ready to depart from Strabane for Stranorlar for the 14.29 on Saturday 9th September 1958.

Activity at Strabane

At 15.00 the Stranorlar goods, which had been standing in the Stranorlar loop, departed. This comprised Loco 5, Drumboe, Vans 268(H), 89(S), 260(H), 83(H), Trucks 222, 119, 211, and Vans 195(S), 12(H), 38(H), 86(S), 247(C), 73(S), 269(H), 2(C), and Brake compo 28. Loco 2, Blanche, with its train from Letterkenny, was then able to access the goods yard.

At 15.50, Railbus 19 and Mailvan arrived from Letterkenny. Then I climbed up into Coach 30 on the afternoon goods to Letterkenny, which was standing in the Letterkenny line loop. We departed five minutes later behind Loco 2. As well as coach 30, there were Vans 190(S), 17, 192(S), trucks 115, 227, 236, and another (I couldn't see the number) with Brake compo 53 bringing up the rear.

Above: No 2, Blanche, bringing the Letterkenny goods into Strabane bunker first at 14.43 on Saturday 9th September 1958.

Below: No 5 Drumboe taking the Stranorlar goods at 15.00 on 9th September 1958 as described above.

Activity at Strabane

We passed the ½ mile post at 15.57, and arrived at Lifford at 15.57 30secs. After some shunting which included adding Vans 189(S), 77(S), 283(H), 240(C), 84(S), and 243(C) we left Lifford at 16.24. We passed through Ballindrait 2¾ miles at 16.39, 15secs, and reached Raphoe, 6½ mile, at 16.43 30 secs. Here I alighted and the goods waited briefly in the loop till Railbus 18 came through from Letterkenny. I boarded No 18, and we departed at 16.55, and with a six minute stop at Lifford, we reached Strabane at 17.15.

At 17.24, Railbus 15 came in from Stranorlar. Six minutes later, Railbus 19 with three Mailvans, Nos 10, 18, and 17 set off for Letterkenny.

Above: No 2, Blanche, ready to depart from Strabane on the 15.55 mixed train to Letterkenny on which Michael Bunch travelled. Coach 30 behind the engine survives in Derry while Blanche survives at the museum in Cultra, Belfast.

Below: An unusual view from the rear of a goods train in Lifford looking towards Letterkenny. The next station down this straight line is Ballindrait.

Activity at Strabane

Then as I was preparing to catch a GNR train back to Derry, I saw GNR railcar "A" coming in from the south, and thought that it was the 18.15, running early. I had never seen this vehicle before on the Derry line. However enquiry revealed that it was terminating at Strabane and returning to Omagh. I thought it was worth getting a ride in this old vehicle, so got a ticket to Victoria Bridge, and boarded.

Railcar "A" was used widely throughout the GNR in its later days and today it was apparently on a test run. As there were no other passengers, the guard took me into the engine compartment, to see the above floor engine. We were soon at Victoria Bridge, so after a quick look around there, I had to catch a bus back to Derry.

Above: Railcar 19 in the Letterkenny platform at Strabane Station, ready to form the 17.30 to Letterkenny. The train will be formed of the railcar itself and three red vans. Railcar 19 is still extant, though not in use, on the Isle of Man.

Below: 15-ton bogie wagon no 334, a purchase from the Clogher Valley Railway redundant stock in 1941.

CDR CLOSURE PROPOSALS

Early 1959

During this next few months, I read of the threats to close first the Ballyshannon branch, and ultimately the whole system - despite the busy look of the railway system in the pictures that I had taken. I wrote to Mr B L Curran, who had been manager of the CDRJC since the death of Henry Forbes in 1943, to see what I could find out.

I had a nice reply, to the effect that no closure date had yet been set. He explained that since the 30th September 1958 the Joint Committee now was entirely Irish, comprising three each members from the UTA and the CIE. He also listed the current rolling stock, which still included 7 steam locos (though I knew 2 were out of use), 1 diesel tractor (Phœnix), 8 oil powered motor vehicles (the Railcars 10, 12, 14, 15, 16, 18, 19, & 20), 18 passenger carriages (3 less than in 1956), 3 trailer coaches, 15 other coaching vehicles, 63 open wagons, and 173 covered vans. Although this all seemed very healthy, I had not realised I would never travel on another CDR service train again.

At that time in early 1959, the steam loco list consisted of No 1 Alice, No 2 Blanche, No 3 Lydia, No 4 Meenglas, No 5 Drumboe, No 6 Columbkille and No 11 Erne. Of these it was the two Class 5A locos, Alice and Lydia, that were out of use in Stranorlar. All the other locos were in regular use.

I then read in the Londonderry Sentinel, that at a meeting on February 24th 1959 involving the Eire Minister of Industry and Commerce, with the Northern Ireland Minister of Commerce, the closure of the CDR has been ratified.

Two Statutory Instruments were published by the Stationary Office in Dublin, No 178 of 1959, relating to the line from Donegal to Ballyshannon, and No 179, relating to the rest of the system, as is situated in the County of Donegal.

This was the start of the final removal of the largest narrow gauge system in the British Isles.

FINAL BOXING IN AT VICTORIA ROAD

3rd August 1960

By now the whole CDR system had closed but I found time first to have a look to see how the work was progressing at Victoria Road. The platform area was now completely boxed in, with a single door on to the rest of the platform. The platforms themselves were still clearly extant. There were to be some more narrow gauge trains here during a revival period in the 1970s but the trains were finally removed with the help of Lord O'Neill to Shanes Castle before coming back in the 1990s to the Foyle Valley Museum on the other side of the river. That museum is now itself defunct but it is hoped that the Destined organisation now resident there will be able to revive things.

Below: The completed boxing in of Victoria Road Station in August 1960 which retained the original roofing canopy. Compare with the pictures on page 73.

FIRST REVISIT TO THE CDR AFTER CLOSURE

4th August 1960

I had not been able to visit Strabane for a couple of years, and in that time the CDR closed on 31st December 1959. Now that the railway was closed, I came back for a sentimental look around. Although the CDR station was closed to rail traffic, there was still some stock on the south-east side of the station.

However, on the Letterkenny side, the lines have been removed and the track bed made into a narrow road right round to Lifford. Loco 5, Drumboe, and coach 23 were parked in the sidings at the south end of the station, and a selection of goods stock was also seen.

Above: Stock on the south-east side of Strabane Station on 4th August 1960. Some stored rails and a number of goods vehicles are evident, plus at right centre Loco No 5, Drumboe, can be seen. The footbridge crossing from the CDR to the GNR still exists as does the 'pagoda' roof southern CDR signal box on the left.

Below: The strange sight of the line to Letterkenny still with starter signal and signal box, but with tarmac replacing the rails to allow buses to access the railway bridge over the Foyle, thus permitting these heavy vehicles to cross the river prior to the rebuilding of the road bridge on the main road. Note the water tank and Camel's Hump bridge are still very much in existence at this time at centre right.

First revisit to the CDR after closure

At this time in August 1960, the GNR line to Derry was still open and would remain so until early 1965. Here in Strabane the access road to the closed CDR part of the station now continues on beside the original Letterkenny platform and then crosses over the remains of the Derry branch to reach the tranship shed, so that the CDR lorries can be loaded from the GNR trains which still run.

Although the CDR have closed the railway part of its operation, its lorries and buses are still running. The CDR buses can reach the station via the old access road down from the Camel's Hump and buses not actually in service can actually park on the former Letterkenny platform, as can be seen in the picture that I took below.

Above: P267 and two other CIE buses in CDR livery parked on the old Letterkenny platform at Strabane.
Below: CIE bus P214 in CDR livery at Strabane station on 4th August 1960 after closure of the CDR. Note the CDR crest on the side of this bus.

First revisit to the CDR after closure

I then walked along the new road laid on the old railway track over the old railway bridge to Lifford station area. Between the bridge and the original station this new road turned off to join the existing road network west of the River Foyle.

I was surprised to see that after this point the rails remained through the station and on towards Letterkenny. I walked down to the western extent of the station and took a picture back from the Letterkenny side of Lifford Station.

Above: The river bridge at Lifford looking back towards Strabane showing the tarmac surface laid for the roadway. The old railway bridge provided the route across the river for buses and heavy lorries until the new existing road bridge was built in 1964.

Below: Proof that the rails still remained at Lifford in August 1960 in this view looking towards Lifford from the Letterkenny side. These rails would soon be gone.

First revisit to the CDR after closure

Returning to Strabane, I caught a bus to Stranorlar. It almost seemed as if I was in a railbus, as I went round the curve, and over the bridge to Lifford, but I missed the noise of metal wheels on railjoints, and the clanking of the coupling rods. We then headed west and I alighted by the station at Stranorlar.

Permission to have a look round was granted at the office, so I was able to walk up and down the sidings, and log the numbers of all the stock.

The sidings were all crammed full of stock awaiting disposal. At this time very little had been disposed of, and I found that Locos 1, 2 and 3 were still in the engine shed. No 6 was in the General Stores along with Railbus 12. The rest of the railbuses were here, except No 16. There were no seats in No 14. Phoenix, which had been used on lifting the line between Raphoe and Lifford was here. Trailer 3 was also here.

Above: Railcar 14 awaiting disposal at Stranorlar having already lost its seats.
Below: Trailer 3 at Stranorlar. This was not sold off, but was preserved and is now on show at the museum in Cultra, Belfast.

All the remaining coaches were here except 23 which was at Strabane as previously noted. I was able to get in Coach 59, and took a picture of the interior. Amongst the coaches were nos 30 and 58 which have subsequently been saved. Also there was the unique 1893 Oldbury Coach 13 with two saloons and a single central compartment. Reputedly this ended its days in Rossnowlagh as a chalet but I have not found any further evidence for this. Apart from the coaches there were 124 assorted goods vehicles demonstrating the size of the railway and its loss to Donegal and enthusiasts.

Above: The interior of Coach 59 - one of the three coaches that came from the NCC originally with lighting, corridor connections and toilets. The latter two were removed on arrival at the CDR.

Below: Another of the three luxury coaches that came from the NCC in 1950, Coach 58, awaiting sale at Stranorlar. This proved too long for easy removal and so was cut into two, becoming two holiday chalets in different parts of Donegal. Remarkably, both halves were eventually recognized and were finally reassembled at Donegal Town Station where the restored body of Coach 58 is now on show.

Above: Coach 23 (left) and Coach 58 at Stranorlar. Note the significantly lower and wider cross-section of No 58 as one of the luxury ex-NCC vehicles.
Below: Coach 13 (left) and Coach 30 at Stranorlar. Note the roof vents over the doors at each and and in the centre of Coach 13. The end doors led to the two saloons, and the centre door to the single centre compartment. Coach 30 was delivered with end windows and as a kind of "observation" coach was always popular as a railcar trailer. It survived and was restored and is stored at the defunct Foyle Valley Railway museum now run by Destined.

Above: Close-up of coach 30 in the yard at Stranorlar showing the CDRJC logo and number.
Below: A view which gives an idea of the amount of stock stored for disposal in Stranorlar yard. Here we are looking past some spare goods stock to the passenger vehicles. A sad sight given how these vehicles enabled the railway to give such good service to the community over many years.

Road to Lifford ⟶

The Camel's
Hump bridge

53

15

Goods
Shed

16

56

40

47

17

12

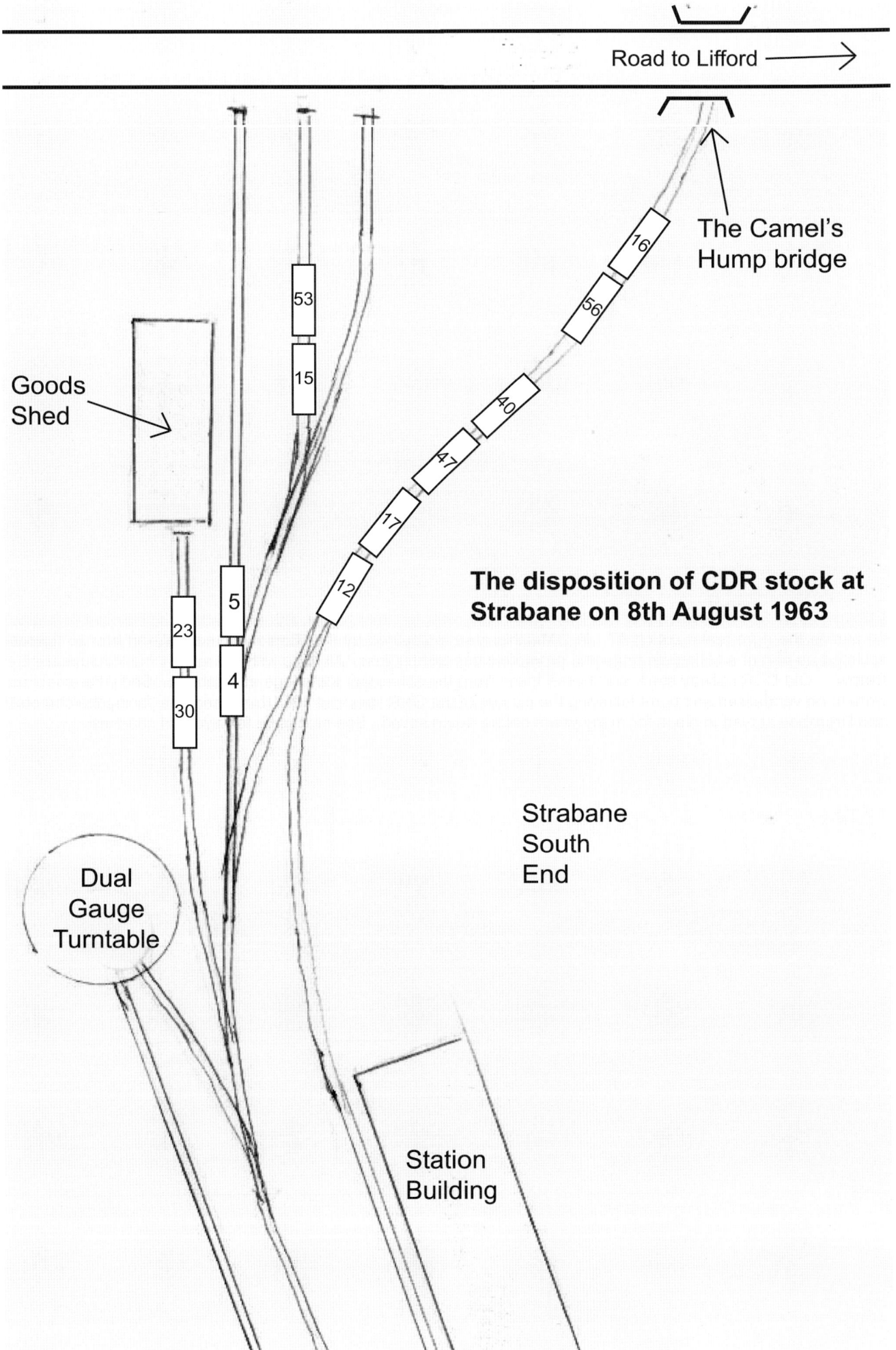

**The disposition of CDR stock at
Strabane on 8th August 1963**

5

23

4

30

Strabane
South
End

Dual
Gauge
Turntable

Station
Building

Above: The north of Strabane Station with rails now lifted on the CDR part of the site, with sleepers stacked on the trackbed. The platform is being used to park staff cars but it seems the customs tables are still in place.
Below: Looking south from the north side of Strabane Station, with the operational GNR shown on the left.

CDR stock repainted and surviving

After my exploration of Strabane Station, I caught the CDR bus to Stranorlar, and had a look around. Apart from the piles of dismantled track and a few goods vans, the main item of interest was a railbus. It was un-numbered, but appeared to me to be the tractor from No 16, with the trailer from No 15. This would not have been so unusual, as to allow general maintenance the articulated trailers were often swapped onto different tractors.

Further research to check the differing window design of the articulated passenger trailers shows that my assumption was right. The body of Trailer 15 still survives, restored, at Donegal Town.

Above & Below: Two views of the combination of Railcar 15's trailer with Railcar 16's Tractor in store at Stranorlar in August 1963. They were photographed in the same place eight years later, see page 2. Subsequently the tractor was purchased by a farmer and trace of it has been lost. The Trailer which can be identified by its window type became a holiday home near Donegal Town and then was stored for some 15 years in the local yard of Mr Edwin Kirk before a €6000 Heritage Council Grant allowed a base to be constructed to put it on display and a Donegal Local Development Company grant allowed the restoration of the body which is now used as a display and video room for the Donegal Railway Heritage Centre.

CDR stock repainted and surviving

A further bus ride took me to Letterkenny, where all the running track has now been lifted. This has left loco no 11, Erne, standing all forlorn on a bit of track, and in a horrible green livery. Apparently it has recently been repainted in this colour, perhaps in an attempt to match Swilly livery, or perhaps to protect the metal, or a bit of both.

I was to learn later that Erne stayed in this position until 1967 when for some reason it was scrapped apparently without any formal permission for this having been given. Something of a mystery surrounds this loss of an important piece of Irish narrow gauge railway heritage. That was the last I saw of Erne..

Below: My last picture of Erne, her tracklifting work finished, now abandoned in the yard at Letterkenny, and treated to a coat of bright green paint.

CDR STOCK STILL SURVIVING

Summer 1964

I had a quick visit to Strabane, date unknown, to find that the situation was little changed from last year. All the track is now lifted apart from the few short lengths on which the stock is standing. Otherwise all looked in good condition ready for re-creation of a railway - but the adjacent GNR, as guardian, was to close in February 1965..

B L CURRAN RETIRES

May 1966

I read in the paper, that Mr B L Curran, manager of the CDRJC since the death of Henry Forbes in 1943, retired on the 31st of the month. He has been replaced as manager, by Mr Fitzgerald, previously the Galway area manager of CIE. The new secretary will be Mr. Hayes, also ex CIE. A Mr Dunnion, with 22 years service with the CDR, is to become an executive officer.

Above: Summer 1964 at Strabane. Left to right, Locos 4, Meenglas, and 5, Drumboe, with Coaches 30 and 23 with guard's ducket. Coach 30 has survived but 23 did not although its twin No 28 is at Donegal Town in 2018.
Below: The line-up of coaches at Strabane in 1964. Left to right are Numbers 16, 56, 40, 47, 17 & 12.

DESTRUCTION AND VANDALISM

July 1966

I came to Strabane by bus, as the GNR line from Derry to Belfast via Strabane had closed in February last year. Quite unlike the hopeful previous scene with repainted locos and coaches, there is a scene of total devastation. The Strabane station footbridge is being dismantled, as are the two railway bridges over the rivers, on the lines to Stranorlar and to Lifford. The Lifford railway bridge over the Foyle has now been superseded by a new road bridge, over which the CDR buses and lorries can cross to get into Donegal. The CDR buses now run right in to Strabane town, given that the GNR station is closed. Worse, however, is the state of the former CDR rolling stock, which is seriously vandalised. All the windows have been broken. The remaining rails have been pulled out from under the coaches, and the stock is just standing on the bare earth.

After all the efforts by Dr Cox to purchase a working selection of equipment and its successful storage and maintenance for several years, this comes as a severe shock and a loss that cannot be reversed. Although there were people who were concerned, and who had some success in saving items, it was a great pity that there was insufficient overall interest in saving the railway to prevent what we see here happening.

Above: After the joy of seeing the remaining CDR locos and stock in such good apparent condition tidily lined up at Strabane Station as late as 1964, it was a shock to see the difference in 1966. The closure of the GNR part of the station in February 1965 has allowed over a year of theft and vandalism which has had a disastrous effect on the condition of the stock as can be seen in this photo. As time went on things were only to get worse, and it would not be long before first there was no glass left in the window openings, and then no doors left in the coaches. That was before the use of the matchboarding for firewood.

Right: Coach 23 in early 1970 with the Goods Shed behind at Strabane. The glass has all gone as have all the doors including the central ones of the guard's compartment, On the footboard are some of the 1969 built 5.5 mm to the foot models made by Neil Tee, including Coach 23 itself (furthest left), that are now on show at the Donegal Railway Heritage Centre. Photo by Neil Tee

Above: Strabane Station in July 1966 with the well-known footbridge now part demolished. The station buildings themselves survived a few more years and were still present in 1971.
Below: Lifford Station on the same day as the above picture. By 2018, very little had changed here since the operating days of the railway.

Above: The remains of the bridge over the Mourne just south of Strabane on the line to Stranorlar.
Below: The remains of the railway bridge at Lifford over the Foyle. Since closure of the railway. this had proved vital for carrying heavy coach and goods traffic until a new bridge was built on the main road.

DEMISE & REVIVAL BATTLE EACH OTHER.......................
DEPRESSION AT STRABANE

Summer 1968

I passed through Strabane today, but didn't take any photos as the whole scene was too depressing. The two locos are still basically intact, but all that remains of the coaches now is a line of chassis. Every part of them that was wooden has been removed by the gypsies camped on the site, who presumably found the coaches a marvellous source of firewood.

DEMOLITION AT STRANORLAR

January 1972

I read that the Station buildings at Stranorlar are being demolished. The townspeople are hoping that the clock can be saved.

REVIVAL AT VICTORIA ROAD

July 1972

There was a big bit in the Derry Sentinel, concerning the restoration of some track at Victoria Road by the North West of Ireland Railway Society. Agreement has been reached with the owners of the land to lay some track, with the aim of reaching along the old track bed, which is still intact as far as Prehen. The starter signal at the end of the platform has been restored to working order. This did turn out to be a revival but only a temporary respite, before a move to Shane's Castle under the auspices of Lord O'Neill.

MOVE TO SHANE'S CASTLE

18th May 1981

Today, I had a letter from Lord O'Neill, in reply to an enquiry from me. In December 1978, Locomotive No. 6, Coach 14, Railcars 12 and 18, and one red wagon were removed from Victoria Road, and taken to Shane's Castle. Five coach chassis were collected from Strabane, and also taken to Shane's Castle. He added that most of this stock still belongs to Dr Cox. The North West of Ireland Railway Society is hoping to come to an agreement with Dr Cox to use the stock in a new scheme at Derry.

FOYLE VALLEY RAILWAY MUSEUM

20th October 2008

I had my first visit to Derry for forty years, having to attend a funeral. As we passed over Craigavon Bridge, I saw a flash of red. It was one of the CDR 2-6-4 tanks standing all forlorn outside the shed of the closed Foyle Valley Railway building, on the site of the former GNR goods yard. This was Class 5 Loco No 4 Meenglas which was to stand there another 10 years before going for a much needed cosmetic restoration in 2018. A good proportion of £1 million was apparently spent on this Foyle Valley Railway Museum, built on the old trackbed of the Great Northern Railway on the west bank of the Foyle opposite Victoria Road station. I learned that Railcars 12 & 18 were restored and did indeed run trains here for some years, but this museum was itself non-operational by 2001.

So as my diary notes of the County Donegal end, there are some questions we might all ask ourselves. After the depressing scenes I saw at Strabane, there was apparently a successful revival of the railway for a while at Victoria Road, and then after stock moved for a while to Shane's Castle with the help of Lord O'Neill. A new operation was set up at the Foyle Valley Railway Museum on the west bank of the Foyle and then that seemed to be condemned to a demise like the initial efforts at Strabane with Dr Cox, and then all the other attempts at revival.

THE UPS & DOWNS OF REVIVAL

2018 & a summary of events since the 1960s

I wondered how all described on this page happened and made some enquiries. The results of these allow me to give, at the end of this book, a summary of what happened from the restoration and revival point of view after the initial disappointment with decay of stock at Strabane in the mid 1960s. The County Donegal Railway revivals seem to go in waves where all goes well for a while and then decline sets in again. For example, the defunct Foyle Valley Railway Museum is now in 2018 in the hands of a new group, Destined. This organisation will hopefully be able to revive the museum and the rolling stock there including locos Meenglas, Columbkille, Railcar 12 & Coach 14. The summary is prepared with the help of Neil Tee, for many years involved with the Donegal Railway Heritage Centre at Donegal Town, and George Haire, a long-term committee member of the North West of Ireland Railway Society, a past Chairman of County Donegal Railway Restoration Ltd, and a co-author of the publication *Railway Days in Strabane*.

Before this summary, I am adding in the photos and notes I had about the Londonderry Port and Harbour Commissioners lines. These had dual gauge sidings and thus were able to accommodate wagons and vans from the 3 foot gauge lines. By coincidence the photo taken of the sidings on Page 108 shows exactly the location where, about a quarter century after the picture was taken, the Foyle Valley Museum was built, on the old Great Northern Railway land, to house some of the remaining County Donegal Railway locos, stock and artefacts.

The Future

Although this completes my own diary, I suspect that and indeed hope that the story is not over yet.

LONDONDERRY PORT & HARBOUR COMMISSIONERS

The town of Derry developed swiftly during the 1860s, partially aided by the railways, both standard and narrow gauge. As far as the docks were concerned, these developed into two miles of quays which were supported by a railway system with its own yard under the supervision of the Londonderry Port & Harbour Commissioners.

To facilitate the movement of goods in the burgeoning port the railway system provided interconnection with all four of the railways at that time bringing traffic into their terminal stations in Derry. These were:

- the line along the Antrim Coast from the east with its terminus at Waterside, for many years under the jurisdiction of the NCC
- the line from Clones and Omagh with its terminus at Foyle Road, under the jurisdiction of the Great Northern Railway of Ireland
- The County Donegal Railway with its terminus at Victoria Road
- The Londonderry & Lough Swilly Railway with its terminus at Graving Dock.

The first two were laid to the 5 feet 3 inch Irish standard gauge and the latter two were the were the narrow three foot gauge.

The secret to the interlinking was the dual gauge track laid on the Port Commissioners lines. These linked the stations on each side of the river but there was also a dual gauge link from east to west across the river by dual gauge tracks laid on the lower deck of the Craigavon Bridge. There were small turntables at each end of the Craigavon bridge big enough for railway wagons and trucks to be turned and shunted across the bridge, although locos and bigger vehicles were not able to pass this way. In fact locos were built and operated by the Port Commissioners with buffer and coupling arrangements to suit both gauges. As shown in the following photographs a shunting tractor was also frequently used.

The Port railway system survived the two narrow gauge lines but was closed in 1962 while the broader gauge lines were still operational.

As far as I can remember, the photos of the mixed gauge track were taken while I was still stationed in Derry, so would have been in 1955 or 1956, but certainly after Victoria Road station was closed. I think it was in the winter of 1956 that owing to the icy conditions, one of the steam engines was used. I could see it from HMS Sea Eagle directly across the river. It was midweek and as I was on duty and was unable to get away. By the weekend the weather had improved, and the tractors were in use again. The photos may have been taken then as I had gone across with my camera.

Below: Dual gauge track with a shunting tractor at work on the lines operated by the Londonderry Port & Harbour Commissioners.

Above & Below: Dual gauge track could contain some interesting pointwork and crossovers, much contained within the rather attractive cobbled paving, as shown in these two views. The one above is taken from alongside Foyle Road Station towards the Craigavon Bridge which is visible in the background..

Above: A shunting tractor busy with goods stock on the dual gauge lines on the Londonderry Port & Harbour Commissioners in the 1960s. These were not a commonly seen item on railway jobs although a contemporaneous early 1960s Meccano outfit No 5 came with instructions to build one as model number 18.
Below: More dual gauge pointwork enabling a linkage between the narrow gauge and broad gauge stations in Derry.

THE COUNTY DONEGAL'S UNENDING EPILOGUE.......

FORMATION OF NWIRS

1969-70

On page 104, you will have read that by the late 1960s, the situation at Strabane had become very depressing to look at, especially for those of us who had memories, and photographs, of the railway in full operation. Of course, by this time I had moved away from my job in Derry and was only an occasional and disappointed visitor. So my information on what was going on with ex-County Donegal Railway material has been much supplemented by George Haire, a committee member of North West of Ireland Railway Society that did so much to preserve these items.

However, there were others like myself with memories of the railway and a strong desire to resist the loss to the area of visible manifestations of this major contributor to the development of the industry and population. In 1969, a chance meeting of operatic society members in Ballyliffin, until 1935 a station on the Londonderry & Lough Swilly Railway's extension to Carndonagh, began a special discussion. This lamented the passing of the railways, especially the loss of Erne from Letterkenny (see page 99 and pages 88 & 89 for the last pictures in steam) and the defacing and vandalism of the two County Donegal locos and stock remaining at Strabane (see pages 100, 101 and 115-117 for a recording of their deterioration). The dream was that such disappearance and vandalism might be stopped, and what did remain properly preserved. By 1970, a group of mainly local enthusiasts had got together and were forming the North West of Ireland Railway Society (NWIRS).

Victoria Road Operation

1973-78

Their search for a location for holding their meetings and items which could be put together to form a small museum resulted, in an amazing piece of good fortune at that time, in gaining space in part of the what was the old County Donegal Railway Station at Victoria Road in Derry. This was thanks to the commercial operation O'Neill & McHenry wholesale grocers then resident in the old Victoria Road Station. Meetings at that location began in 1972 and by 1973 there was an official opening of a section of the premises providing a meeting place and a museum.

Once a base had been established, NWIRS began the consideration of whether remaining items of operational rolling stock could be brought to Victoria Road and displayed or even operated for the public. The museum had proved popular in attracting significant numbers of visitors since the 1973 opening. Effort concentrated on clearing the station site in the area between the station buildings and the east bank of the Foyle where the transfer sidings had been.

The main items of rolling stock remaining consisted of Class 5 loco "Columbkille", Railcars 12 & 18, a Coach and a goods van all kept at Stranorlar following the auction there in the early 1960s. Their location was the original railway sheds, which were now in a parlous condition and beginning to collapse. For some reason there was no record of a need to move Railcar 16 coupled to Trailer 15 which was still there outside in 1971 but must have moved shortly afterwards. Also under consideration were the two other Class 5 locos Meenglas and Drumboe which had been languishing at Strabane since the closure of the County Donegal line, receiving considerable attention from vandals over the years since the closure of the Great Northern line in February 1965.

Dr Cox

1960 onwards

Dr Ralph Cox was born in Pittsburgh in 1919 and graduated from the university there as a dentist. While this appeared a good career, it was during a while in the Navy that Dr Cox became passionate about aviation and this led eventually to him founding an airline. He developed this into a successful business using World War 1 planes. Later on, the progress of the US version of Health & Safety effectively put an end to the operation of this for the public and severely affected his finances. He had other passions and interests, one being classic cars which he collected, and another interest was the idea of setting up a narrow gauge railway near his home in the US which was New Jersey by the time of the County Donegal's closure. Millionaire Dr Cox heard tell of the demise of the Donegal and became interested in the idea of purchasing sufficient of the remains to take back to New Jersey to form a small narrow gauge operational railway there.

As a result on hearing of the disposal of the stock he made several purchases of the remaining locos and vehicles. By the time of the disposal auction in March 1961, he had become the owner of Class 5 locos Columbkille, Drumboe and Meenglas, Class 4 Erne, Railcars 12, 16 & 18, some 10 coaches and a quantity of wagons and wagon chassis plus rails, points and other equipment. It all looked very hopeful that a mini-County Donegal would be recreated in the US.

This was not to be. By the late 1960s, as we have seen, Meenglas and Drumboe had suffered from both weather and vandals at Strabane, and really only the chassis were left of the coaches there. The other equipment stored at Stranorlar was originally under cover but the buildings were now in a poor state and giving less safety from elements and damage. The reason given for stock remaining at Stranorlar and Strabane was the cost of shipping to the US. It might be a little difficult to reconcile this being a complete block to progress when Alan Pegler was moving Flying Scotsman to the US, and there was such a large amount of items of value in the Cox collection. Nevertheless, this outcome must have been as much of a disappointment to Dr Cox himself as to observers seeing the decline of the potentially saveable railway items.

The misery was prolonged even further by the fact that Dr Cox, resident some 3000 miles way, owned the deteriorating items and even if genuine efforts were made by enthusiasts to save items their contributions were in danger of only adding value to the Cox estate rather than enabling a repurchase for conservation in Ireland or the UK. The repercussions of this are still being felt in 2018.

Dr Cox made a visit to Derry in 1974 and after discussions he made a major contribution to facilitating a solution to this tricky issue. An agreement was signed to hand over Railcar 18, loco Drumboe and five of the coach chassis from Strabane to NWIRS. It was still hoped that a railway could be set up in the USA, and to avoid further deterioration of the other items, these were allowed to be brought to Victoria Road.

These were loco Columbkille, Railcar 12, Coach 14 and Red Van 19. With around 200 members, NWIRS was now hoping it could achieve a position where all the stock could in fact eventually be purchased from Dr Cox, who lived to the great age of 97 but never managed to set up his narrow gauge line in the US. Reputedly Dr Cox had agreed that if he had not been able to collect his rolling stock by a certain date – believed in one agreement to be July 1981 – then ownership would pass to NWIRS. However, there was always some doubt about ownership of some of the stock leading later to endless arguments between NWIRS and Derry City Council about this, as Derry City Council saw themselves as guardians of the Cox stock.

Victoria Road Develops
1974-78
Between 1974 and 1976 track was laid at Victoria Road where the old transfer sidings had been for movement of goods between the 3 foot and 5 foot 3 inch gauges. Two sidings joined by a point resulted and by 1976 a lean-to had been added to the riverbank side of the old station buildings to house Railcars 12 & 18 to assist in their conservation and help protect any restoration done.

An intriguing plan was produced which would have seen the 3 foot gauge line extended south from Victoria Road along the old trackbed as far as the then new Everglades hotel at Prehen. Here there was sufficient land between the old formation and the river bank at Riverside Park to create a loop to allow trains to reverse direction and travel back towards Victoria Road. This creative and major effort by the NWIRS to produce a viable plan also included persuading the full Derry City Council to back the idea as also did the Northern Ireland Tourist Board. This was the initial idea for a Foyle Valley Railway. At that time it was hoped that the Foyle Valley Railway's first stage of development would actually happen in 1977.

At the same time, as part of its fund generation activities, the NWIRS was arranging Day Excursion trains out of Derry with Northern Ireland Railways, suitably entitled the Foyle Enterprise, having developed an effective working relationship with the operational railway.

Having read this far, readers could be forgiven for building up an impression that there really was going to be a revived railway going south from Victoria Road station. This was not to happen although it might well have been a cheaper alternative long-term option than the expensive Foyle Valley Railway museum that was eventually created on the West bank of the river. The NWIRS reports in their Starter magazine reflect that Derry City Council was somewhat slow to react to what looked like an exciting prospect to railway and tourism enthusiasts, although grant aid was expected to be available for the proposed Foyle Valley Railway project.

What really shocked the whole set of arrangements was the news that the grocers O'Neill & McHenry who had occupied Victoria Road Station were retiring from business and were to be liquidated. This could have worked two ways. It might have indicated the unique opportunity for Derry City Council to step in and purchase the site, and making use of the grants available, assist in the set-up of the proposed revived railway to Prehen. The other option was the demise of the whole scheme.

Despite what enthusiasts might rightly have hoped that a huge opportunity existed for the restoration of a short length of the County Donegal on one of its original formations, the opportunity for revival was missed. Worse, notice was effectively served on NWIRS that all their equipment and stock on site at Victoria Road would have to be moved - a sad reward for the huge amount of work that members of NWIRS had put in.

Shane's Castle
1979-1986
It was at this point that Lord O'Neill stepped in to offer help by allowing the storage of all the Victoria Road stock at Shane's Castle in Antrim. There was very little notice given to the NWIRS of the need to move stock and the move took place in December 1978. There was already a small operational 3 foot gauge line at Shane's Castle and after a while it became possible to run the Donegal stock along this. Lord O'Neill also obtained planning permission for a storage building for the Donegal items and got this erected. A further part of his valuable support was that he obtained a quote to move locos Meenglas and Drumboe from Strabane where they now stood on ground that was part of the military border guard arrangement, perhaps helping to avoid further theft from them.

Unfortunately Shane's Caste was located in Antrim, some distance away, and this did provide a travel obstacle to a significant number of the active Derry-based supporters of NWIRS. A small number of dedicated members did continue regular visits to sell NWIRS items such as souvenirs, and others plus a lot of the general public were attracted by open days run at Shane's a couple of times a year.

Once the railcars were in use on the one and a half mile Shane's Castle track, the opportunity was apparently taken to give them a good run. A frequent driver was the late Joe Curran, son of the last General Manager of the CDR (see page 100). George Haire recalls these were the fastest journeys he had ever made on the railcars which he himself drove later on in the 1990s at the Foyle Valley Railway Museum. He reckoned 40mph was reached on the well-laid track at Shane's Castle.

The Foyle Valley Railway Museum
1985-2000

Derry City Council had meanwhile employed an architect to advise on where a museum to replace that at Victoria Road should best be located once funding and grant aid were available. It was finally agreed that this site should be on the old trackbed of the Great Northern Railway on the opposite side of the river from Victoria Road (See page 108).

The buildings were completed in 1986 and initially about a mile of track was laid along the old trackbed southwards towards Carrigans which lay across the border in Donegal and, with St Johnston, was a target for the rails to reach. The old Great Northern trackbed was undisturbed up to these points and indeed had been classified as a public footpath by Derry City Council for the part running within the County of Derry.

The new buildings beside the Craigavon Bridge were comprehensive, consisting of platforms for trains to be run, a public viewing area, a retail shop, a conference room and workshops.The Foyle Valley Railway Museum was formally opened in May 1989.

Initially Railcar 12 was used with a Simplex shunter purchased by the Council from Shane's Castle. The two were connected by a drawbar so the Railcar would lead on the trip out from the museum, and the shunter could pull Railcar 12 in reverse for the return trips. While County Donegal Railcars could reverse for shunting duties, they were not intended to travel long distances in reverse, and this arrangement overcame the problem as the railcar would be travelling backwards out of gear. For a while passengers were carried by the Simplex towing Railcar Trailer 3 – unmotorised for many years now – and on loan from the museum at Cultra, in Belfast.

At this time Railcar 18 was in store at McCaul's farm, three miles down the line, in a poor state of repair. The NWIRS Treasurer, the late Arthur Thompson, was responsible for raising substantial funding to finance the restoration of both the railcars and

Coach 30, one of those rescued from Strabane. The first spend was on Railcar 18 which was taken to Grimley Brothers of Richill, Armagh and returned restored. After that it was the turn of Railcar 12 which, after 1 million miles of use in its lifetime, went to Willie McCauley of Drumoghill, Co Donegal for restoration.

Its return enabled the two railcars to run back to back to take passengers along the track from the museum towards Carrigans. These passenger runs were greeted by an enthusiastic public. This was topped up by the loan of a steam loco by Michael Kennedy of the Cavan & Leitrim Railway for one week to confirm that steam trains at Derry would be a workable and attractive proposition.

Once again NWIRS seemed to have built up a successful operation which attracted the public both from within Derry and from long distances way, and which preserved an operational example of the County Donegal Railway. However, what began as administrative niggles with Derry City Council grew into major arguments and the Council decided effectively to close the museum from 2001. Although the doors have been open occasionally for visitors and shows, the huge efforts made to open it seem to have gone to waste for over a decade and likewise the opportunities for tourists to see the displays and railcars in operation. At least Railcar No 18 has been in use following a move to Fintown to provide train rides on the Fintown Railway for three miles towards Glenties on the old trackbed from Stranorlar to Glenties. See www.fintownrailway.com.

There is some hope that history will repeat itself with a revival of the Foyle Valley Museum and any necessary make-overs of the County Donegal materials and stock. By 2018, the museum had been taken on by a group called Destined who work with adults who have learning difficulties. It is believed their intention is to relay the track towards Carrigans which has deteriorated seriously over the 18 years of disuse. An initial visible manifestation of activity is that the loco Meenglas, having sat deteriorating outside since the museum was built, has been sent to the Railway Preservation Society of Ireland at Whitehead, Antrim, for cosmetic restoration.*

Donegal Town
1995 onwards

While all the above has happened further north, the Donegal Railway Heritage Centre, which has been open since 1995, continues to provide a year round museum giving details of the history of the railway. Over the years rolling stock has been collected on site, and on display in 2018 were Coaches 28 and 58, Railcar Trailer 5 and the articulated passenger portion of Railcar 15 (see page 98), plus Grey Van 84 and the body of Red Van 12.

* As this book was going to print we heard that Meenglas has been returned to Derry in cosmetically restored condition in January 2019.

Index

Index

Above: Locos No 4, Meenglas, on left, and No 5 Drumboe, on right, as they deteriorate in the weather and vandalism conditions at Strabane in the late 1960s. Note how items such as dome covers and smoke-box door fasteners are visibly missing from Drumboe and the paint renewed in 1963 is fading badly. On the running plate is a set of models of a Donegal loco and coaches made in 5.5 mm to the foot scale in 1969 by Neil Tee and currently on show at the Donegal Railway Heritage Centre. Photo by Neil Tee.

Below: Looking towards Derry through the left spectacle of Meenglas' cab giving a view of the remains of Strabane Station closed some 4 years before. This picture was taken before the dome was stolen. The CDR Station building on left and the GNR signal cabin and canopy still existed but the big footbridge had long gone. There is now in 2018 no trace that there was ever a station here, let alone a major one linking two railway companies. Photo by Neil Tee.

Above: Coaches 15 (left) and 53 in 1970 after all the glass was broken and then the doors were taken, presumably for firewood. It would not be long before only the chassis parts were left. Photo by Neil Tee.
Below: Coach 40 on its way to oblivion in 1970 with all glass and doors now gone. Photo by Neil Tee.